THE LITTLE BOOK OF
THE
TAO TE
CHING

THE LITTLE BOOK OF
THE
TAO TE
CHING

translated by

John R Mabry

ELEMENT

Shaftesbury, Dorset ✧ Rockport, Massachusetts
Brisbane, Queensland

© Element Books Limited 1995

Translation © John R Mabry 1994

First published in Great Britain in 1995 by
ELEMENT BOOKS LIMITED
Shaftesbury, Dorset SP7 8BP

Published in the USA in 1995 by
ELEMENT BOOKS, INC.
PO Box 830, Rockport, MA 01966

Published in Australia in 1995 by
ELEMENT BOOKS LIMITED
for JACARANDA WILEY LIMITED
33 Park Road, Milton, Brisbane 4064

Designed and created by:
The Bridgewater Book Company / Angela Neal
Picture research by Felicity Cox
Printed in Italy by LEGO

British Library Cataloguing in Publication data available

Library of Congress Cataloging
in Publication data available

ISBN 1-85230-707-2

The publishers are grateful to the Ancient Art & Architecture
Collection, the E. T. Archive and the Werner Forman Archive for
permission to reproduce their pictures in this book.

Introduction

WHAT IS THE TAO TE CHING?

The *Tao Te Ching* is a book of Chinese philosophical poetry, written at some time between the 7th and the 4th centuries B.C.E. According to tradition it was written by a quiet librarian named Lao Tzu, which in Chinese can mean, curiously enough, either Old Man or Old Child. Lao Tzu, in his old age, finally gave humanity up as a lost cause. He packed his yak, and headed for the wilderness where things were sane. At the top of a mountain pass, the last outpost of civilization, the gatekeeper persuaded Lao Tzu to commit his philosophy to paper before he left humankind for ever. The resulting book, consisting of just over five thousand Chinese characters, became the famous *Tao Te Ching*, which means 'the book of the Way and its power'.

SO WHAT IS TAOISM?

Alan Watts, in his excellent book *Tao: The Watercourse Way,* offers a simple and sufficient definition: Taoism is 'the way of man's cooperation with the course or trend of the natural world'. That's it. There is nothing inherently spiritual about it. There is nothing in Taoism that relies on some form of divine revelation, nothing that any sensitive human being could not learn simply by observing nature. And that is part of its magic: its simplicity. Lao Tzu was not a man to be impressed by political status or educational degrees. To him, maids or stable boys who were true to their own instincts were the noblest sorts of creatures.

❖

WHY SHOULD WE
BOTHER WITH TAOISM?

Both for personal and global reasons. For the nurturing of our own souls, the *Tao Te Ching* is an unparalleled source of inspiration. From the first few chapters I was entranced by the book's simplicity and awesome profundity, and living with it has seriously affected my life, both spiritually and socially. This is not an uncommon phenomenon, either. Again and again I have watched people who were profoundly touched evolve toward spiritual maturity.

As the world grows smaller, and our ecological pligh grows more severe, it is imperative that we extend our theological feelers and really explore. We need to understand each other, because ignorance breeds fear, and of fear we have had quite enough. It is also very clear that our old ways of thinking and perceiving are not adequate to meet the challenges that our survival will require. We need truly creative approaches, and we should not be afraid to explore new areas.

As John Dunne has written,

> *The holy man of our time, it seems, is not a figure like Gotama [Buddha] or Jesus or Mohammed, a man who could found a world religion, but a figure like Gandhi, a man who passes over by sympathetic understanding from his own religion to other religions and comes back again with new insight to his own. Passing over and coming back, it seems, is the spiritual adventure of our time.*

(*The Way of All the Earth*, MACMILLAN, 1972)

❖

The Tao that can be described in words is not the true Tao
The Name that can be named is not the true Name.

> *From non-existence were called Heaven and Earth*
> *From existence all things were born.*

In being without desires, you experience the wonder
But by having desires, you experience the journey.
Yet both spring from the same source
    and differ mostly in name.

This source is called 'Mystery'
Mystery upon Mystery,
The womb giving birth to all of being.

The Tao is like an empty pitcher,
Poured from, but never drained.
Infinitely deep, it is the source of all things.

It blunts the sharp,
Unties the knotted,
Shades the bright,
Unites with all Dust.

Dimly seen, yet eternally present,
I do not know who gave birth to it,
It is older than any conception of God.

Heaven and Earth are impartial,
They allow things to die.

The Sage is not sentimental,
She knows that all beings must pass away.

The space between Heaven and Earth is like a bellows
Empty, yet inexhaustible
The more it is used, the more it produces.

Trying to explain it will only exhaust you.
It is better to hold on to paradox.

Heaven is eternal, and Earth is long-lasting.
Why are they so enduring?
Because they do not live for themselves.

Therefore the Sage puts himself last
And finds himself in the foremost place.
He does not promote himself, thus he is preserved.

Because he has no thought of 'self',
He is perfectly fulfilled.

The sagely person is like water
Water benefits all things and does not compete with them.

> *It gathers in unpopular places.*
> *In this it is like the Tao.*

In dwelling, live close to the Earth.
In thinking, be open to new ideas. In relationships, be kind.
In speech, tell the truth and keep your word.
In leading people, demonstrate integrity.
In daily matters, be competent.
In acting, consider the appropriate timing.

If you do not try to prove yourself superior to others,
You will be beyond reproach.

Thirty spokes join together at one hub,
But it is the hole in the centre that makes it operable.

Clay is moulded into a pot,
But it is the emptiness inside that makes it useful.

Doors and windows are cut to make a room,
It is the empty spaces that we use.

> *Therefore, existence is what we have,*
> *But non-existence is what we use.*

Look for it and it cannot be seen – it is beyond sight.
Listen for it and it cannot be heard – it is beyond hearing.
Grasp at it and it cannot be caught
    – it is beyond substance.
These three cannot be fully comprehended.

> *They are fundamentally connected*
> *and somehow they are one.*

Its highest isn't bright.
Its lowest isn't dark.
It is infinite!
Continually emerging, completely beyond description,
It returns again and again to nothingness.

If you cling to the Tao of ancient times
    the present will be no problem.
To know the ancient origin is to follow the Tao.

If you can empty yourself of everything,
   you will have lasting peace.
      Things arise, but I contemplate their return.
      Things flourish and grow,
         and then return to their Source.

To return to the Source is to know perfect peace.
I call this a return to Life.

Knowing this Constant, you can embrace all things.
Embracing all things, you can treat them fairly.

❖

Treating them fairly, you are noble.
Being noble, you are like the cosmos.
If you are like the cosmos, you are like the Tao.

   If you are like the Tao, you will have eternal life,
   and you needn't be afraid of dying.

The best leader is one that the people are barely aware of.
The next best is one who is loved and praised by the people.
Next comes one who is feared.
Worst is one who is despised.

> *If the leader does not have enough*
>   *faith in the people,*
> *They will not have faith in him.*

The best leader puts great value in words and says little
So that when his work is finished
The people all say, 'We did it ourselves!'

Forget 'holiness', abandon 'intelligence'
　　and people will be a hundred times better off.
Give up 'humanitarianism', put away 'righteousness'
　　and people will rediscover brotherly love and kindness.
Forget 'great art', throw away 'profit'
　　and there will be no more thieves.
These things are superficial and are simply not enough.
People need something solid to hold on to.

And here it is:
> *Be real.*
> *Embrace simplicity.*
> *Put others first.*
> *Desire little.*

The only virtue worth having is that of following the Tao,
　　and the only thing you can say about the Tao,
　　is that it is elusive and evasive.

It is elusive and evasive, yet it can be observed.
It is evasive and elusive, yet it does manifest itself.
It is dim and dark, yet its essence can be grasped.

> *Its essence is unquestionably genuine.*
> *You can put your faith in it.*

From the beginning of time until the present,
its Name has remained.
In it one can see all of Creation.
How do I know where all of Creation comes from?
I know the Tao!

If you don't want to be broken, bend.
If you want to be straight, allow some crookedness.
If you want to be filled, become empty.
If you want to be made new, let yourself be used.
If you want to be rich, desire little.
Wanting more and more is craziness!

Therefore the sage embraces oneness
    and becomes a model for the world.
Not self-centred, she is enlightened.
Not self-righteous, she is a shining example.
Not self-glorifying, she accomplishes glorious things.
Not boastful, she grows large inside.
She alone does not compete,
And so the world can never overcome her.

When the ancients said, 'If you don't want to be broken, bend'
Were they just uttering empty words?

Bend sincerely and wholeness will return to you.

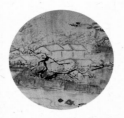

The Tao is Great.
Heaven is Great.
The Earth is Great.
Humankind is also Great.

In the Universe there are
these four things which are Great,
And Humankind is one of them.

Humankind follows the Earth,
The Earth follows Heaven,
Heaven follows the Tao,
And the Tao just acts like itself.

The Sage is always there to help people
So that no one is forsaken.
She is always there to see to things
So that nothing is lost.
This is called being clothed in light.

What is a good person but a bad person's teacher?
What is a bad person but raw material for a good person?

If you do not respect your Teacher,
Or love your 'raw material',
You are greatly confused, regardless of your intelligence.

I call this an essential, yet subtle mystery.

Do you want to own the World and improve it?

I don't think you can.

You see, the World is sacred.
It can't be improved upon.
If you try you will ruin it.
If you try to own it,
You will lose it.

A leader who is advised to rely on the Tao
Does not enforce his will upon the world by military means.
For such things are likely to rebound.

Wherever armies have camped
Thistles and briars grow.
In the wake of war
Bad years are sure to follow.

❖

All weapons are bad news
And all creatures should detest them.
So those who follow the Tao do not keep them.

> *Weapons are the tools of fear.*
> *They are not appropriate for a Sage*
> *And should only be one's last resort.*
> *Peace is always far superior.*

There is no beauty in victory.
To find beauty in it would be to rejoice at killing people.
Anyone who delights in slaughter will never find
 satisfaction in this world.

Military officers should observe their duties gravely.
For when many people are killed
They should be mourned with great sorrow.

Celebrate your victory only with funeral rites.

❖

The great Tao flows everywhere,
  to the left and to the right.
All things rely on it for their life
  and it does not refuse them.
When its work is done, it does not demand recognition.

  It clothes and nourishes all things
  and does not demand allegiance.

Since it makes no demands for itself,
  it can seem to be of small regard.
Yet as all things return to it of their own accord,
  without being commanded, it can truly be regarded Great.
It is only because it does not claim to be Great
That it is able to achieve such Greatness.

Whoever holds firmly to following the Tao
Will draw all the World to herself.
She may go anywhere and not be afraid,
Finding only safety, balance and peace.

Music and good food lure passers-by
But words about the Tao
Seem bland and flavourless to them.

Look, and it cannot be seen.
Listen, and it cannot be heard.
Use it, and it cannot be exhausted.

Returning is the movement of the Tao.
Yielding is the way of the Tao.

The softest thing in the World
Overcomes the hardest thing in the World.
That which is without substance can enter
even where there is no space.

Therefore I know the value of non-action.

Teaching without words
And benefit without actions.
There are few in the World who can grasp it.

True perfection seems flawed
Yet its usefulness is never exhausted.

True fulfilment seems empty
Yet its usefulness is infinite.

True straightness seems crooked,
Great skill appears easy,
Great eloquence sounds awkward.

Cold overcomes heat.
Tranquillity conquers agitation.
Purity and stillness is the universal ideal.

Without going outside,
You can know the whole world.
Without looking out the window,
You can know Heaven's Way.

The further out you seek
The less you understand.

Therefore, the Sage
Knows without needing to travel,
Understands without needing to see,
Accomplishes without 'doing'.

To pursue learning is to grow a little more every day.
To pursue the Tao is to desire a little less every day.

Desire less and less
Until you arrive at 'not-doing'.

When you practise 'not-doing', nothing is left undone.

If you want to have the whole world, have nothing.
If you are always busy doing something,
you cannot enjoy the world.

The Sage's heart is not set in stone.
She is as sensitive to the people's feelings as to her own.

She says, 'To people who are good, I am good.
And to people who are not good? I am good to them, too.'
This is true goodness.

'People who are trustworthy, I trust.
And people who are not trustworthy, I also trust.'
This is real trust.

The Sage who leads harmoniously considers the mind of
     her people as well as her own.
They look to her anxiously.
They are like her own children.

If I possess even a little wisdom
Then while I walk in the light of the Tao
My only fear is that I'll fall into 'doing'.
The path of the Tao is obvious and simple,
But most people prefer to take short-cuts.

> *The courts of law are far from the people's hearts.*
> *The fields are full of weeds,*
> *And the storehouses are empty.*

But look, here are officials in elegant apparel
   carrying sharp swords
Eating and drinking until they are bloated,
Possessed of such wealth that they could never use it all.

> *I call this positively criminal.*
> *It is not the way of the Tao.*

Those who know, do not speak.
Those who speak, do not know.

So shut your mouth
Guard your senses
Blunt your sharpness
Untangle your affairs
Soften your glare
Be one with all dust.
This is the mystery of union.

You cannot approach it
Yet you cannot escape it.
You cannot benefit it
Yet you cannot harm it.
You cannot bestow any honour on it
Yet you cannot rob it of its dignity.
That is why the whole Universe reveres it.

As a leader, lead properly.
Don't resort to force in the usual ways.
Win the World by 'not-doing'.
How do I know to do this?

Listen, the more laws and prohibitions there are
The poorer the people become.
The more dreadful weapons you have
The more chaotic the state of the nation.
The more clever and advanced your knowledge
The stranger things become.
The more commandments and regulations you have
The more thieves there are.

Therefore the Sage who leads says:
'I practise 'not-doing' and the people transform themselves.
I enjoy peace and the people correct themselves.
I stay out of their business affairs and the people prosper.
I have no desires and the people, all by themselves,
    become simple and honest.'

In leading people and
serving Heaven
There is nothing better than moderation.
In moderation, one is already following the Tao.
When one follows the Tao, great goodness is abundant.
When great goodness is in abundance,
There is nothing that cannot be overcome.
When there is nothing that cannot be overcome
Then there are no limits.
Having no limits, one can certainly govern a country.
If you know the country's Mother, you will long endure.

I call this having deep roots and a firm stalk.
This is the Way of long life and great insight.

The Tao is the bosom of the Universe

It is the good person's treasure
And the bad person's refuge.

Flattery may buy one's position
And good deeds can win people over
But if one's heart is not pure
That is all the more reason to cling to the Tao!

Why did the Sages of old value the Tao so much?
Because, when you seek, you find
And when you sin, you are forgiven.

That is why the Tao is the greatest treasure of the Universe.

Do without 'doing'.
Work without forcing.
Taste without seasonings.
Recognize the Great in the small,
And the many in the few.

Repay hatred with kindness.

Deal with the difficult while it is still easy.
Begin great works while they are small.
Certainly the Earth does difficult work with ease,
And accomplishes great affairs from small beginnings.

So, the Sage, by not striving for greatness, achieves greatness.

If you think everything is easy,
You will find only difficulty.

That is why the Sage considers all things difficult
And finds nothing too difficult in the end.

Rivers and the sea are able to rule the streams of a
hundred valleys.
Because they are good at taking the lower position,
The streams of a hundred valleys run to them.

Therefore, if you want to rule effectively over people
You must surely speak as if below them.
If you want to lead well,
You must surely walk behind them.

That way when the Sage takes a position of power
The people will not feel oppressed.
And when the Sage leads
The people will not think he is in the way.

*Therefore the whole world joyfully praises him
and does not tire of him.*

Because he refuses to compete,
The world cannot compete with him.

My words are very easy to understand
And very easy to practise.
Yet the World is not able to understand
Nor able to put them into practice.

My words speak of the primal.
My deeds are but service.
Unless people understand this
They won't understand me.
And since so few understand me,
Then such understanding is rare and valuable indeed.

Therefore the Sage wears common clothes
And hides his treasures only in his heart.

❖

She who knows that she does not know is the best off.
He who pretends to know but doesn't is ill.

Only someone who realizes he is ill can become whole.
The Sage is not ill because she recognizes
   this illness as illness,
Therefore she is not ill.

Who knows why Heaven allows some things to happen?
Even the Sage is stumped sometimes.

The Way of Heaven
Does not compete, but is good at winning;
Does not speak, yet always responds;
Does not demand, but is usually obeyed;
Seems chaotic, but unfolds a most excellent plan.

Heaven's net is cast wide
And though its meshes are loose,
Nothing is ever lost.

When people are alive they are soft and weak.
At their death they are hard and rigid.

All young things, including grass and trees
Are soft and frail.
In death they are withered and dry.

So, all that are hard and rigid take the company of death.
Those who are soft and weak take the company of life.

Therefore, powerful weapons will not succeed
(Remember that strong and tall trees
are the ones that are cut down).

The strong and rigid are broken and laid low.
The soft and weak will always overcome.

Heaven's Way is to take from what has too much
And give it to what does not have enough.
This is not the way of men, however,
    for they take from those who have little
    to increase the wealth of the rich.

So who is it that has too much
and offers it to a needy World?
Only someone who knows the Tao.

Therefore, the Sage works anonymously.
She achieves great things
    but does not wait around for praise.
She does not want her talents to attract attention to her.

In the whole World nothing is softer or weaker than water.
And yet even those who succeed when attacking the hard and
the strong cannot overcome it
Because nothing can harm it.
The weak overcomes the strong.
The soft conquers the hard.

No one in the World can deny this
Yet no one seems to know how to put it into practice.

Therefore the Sage says
'One who accepts a people's shame is qualified to rule it.
One who embraces a condemned people.
is called the king of the Universe.'

True words seem paradoxical.

When enemies are reconciled,
  some resentment invariably remains.
How can this be healed?

Therefore the Sage makes good on his half of the deal
And demands nothing of others.

One who is truly good will keep his promise.
One who is not good will take what he can.

> *Heaven doesn't choose sides*
> *It is always with the good people.*

Let people return to simplicity,
  working with their own hands.
Then they will find joy in their food
Beauty in their simple clothes
Peace in their living
Fulfilment in their traditions.

True words are not beautiful.
Beautiful words are not true.

Good people do not argue.
Argumentative people are not good.

The wise are not necessarily well-educated.
The well-educated are not necessarily wise.

> *The Sage does not hoard things.*
> *The more she does for others*
> *The more she finds she has.*
> *The more she gives to others*
> *The more she finds she gains.*

Heaven's Way is to nourish, not to harm.
The Sage's Way is to work, yet not compete.